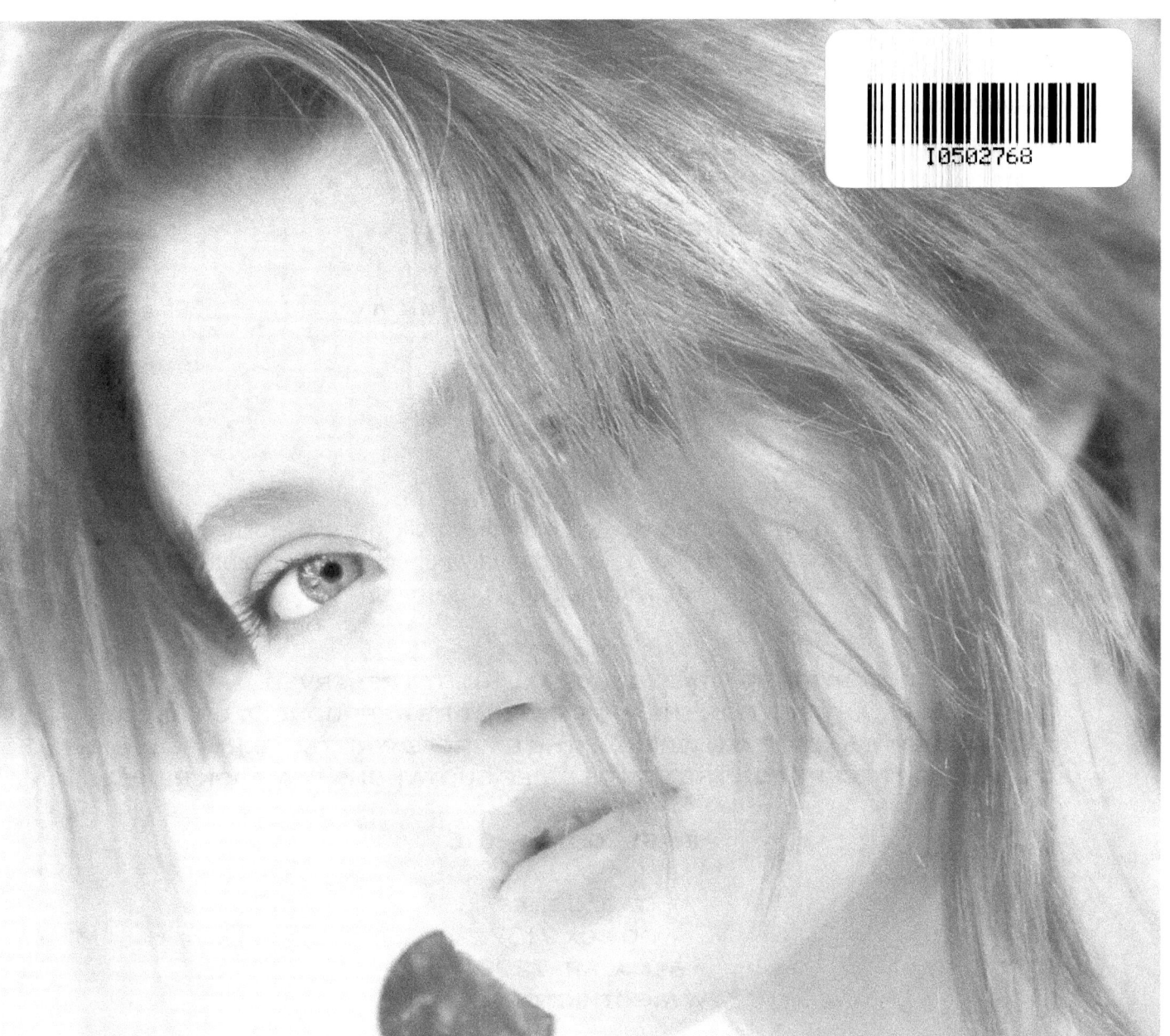

Women of Fashion
grayscale coloring book

curated by

Tabz Jones

Women of Fashion

grayscale coloring book

curated by

Tabz Jones

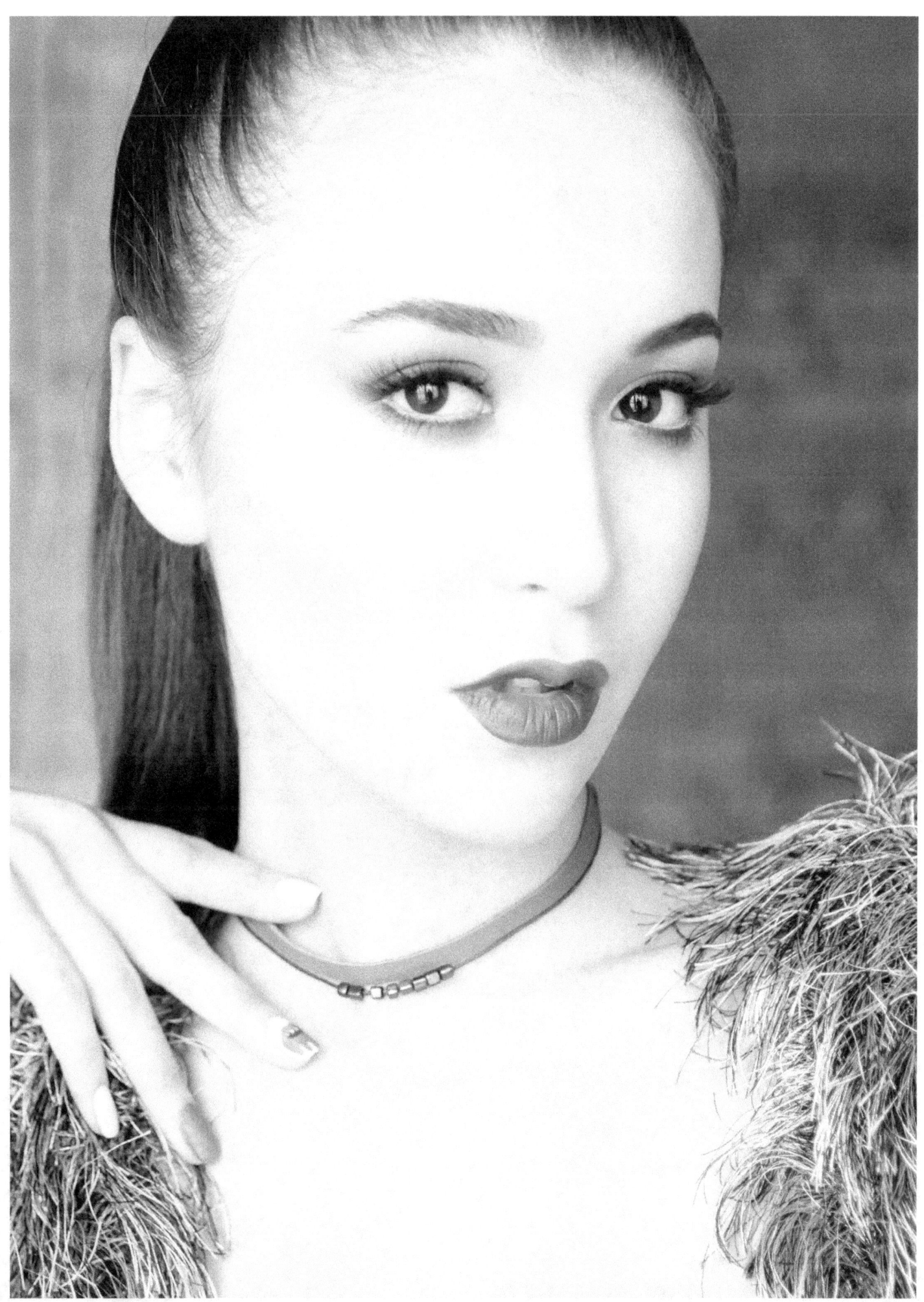

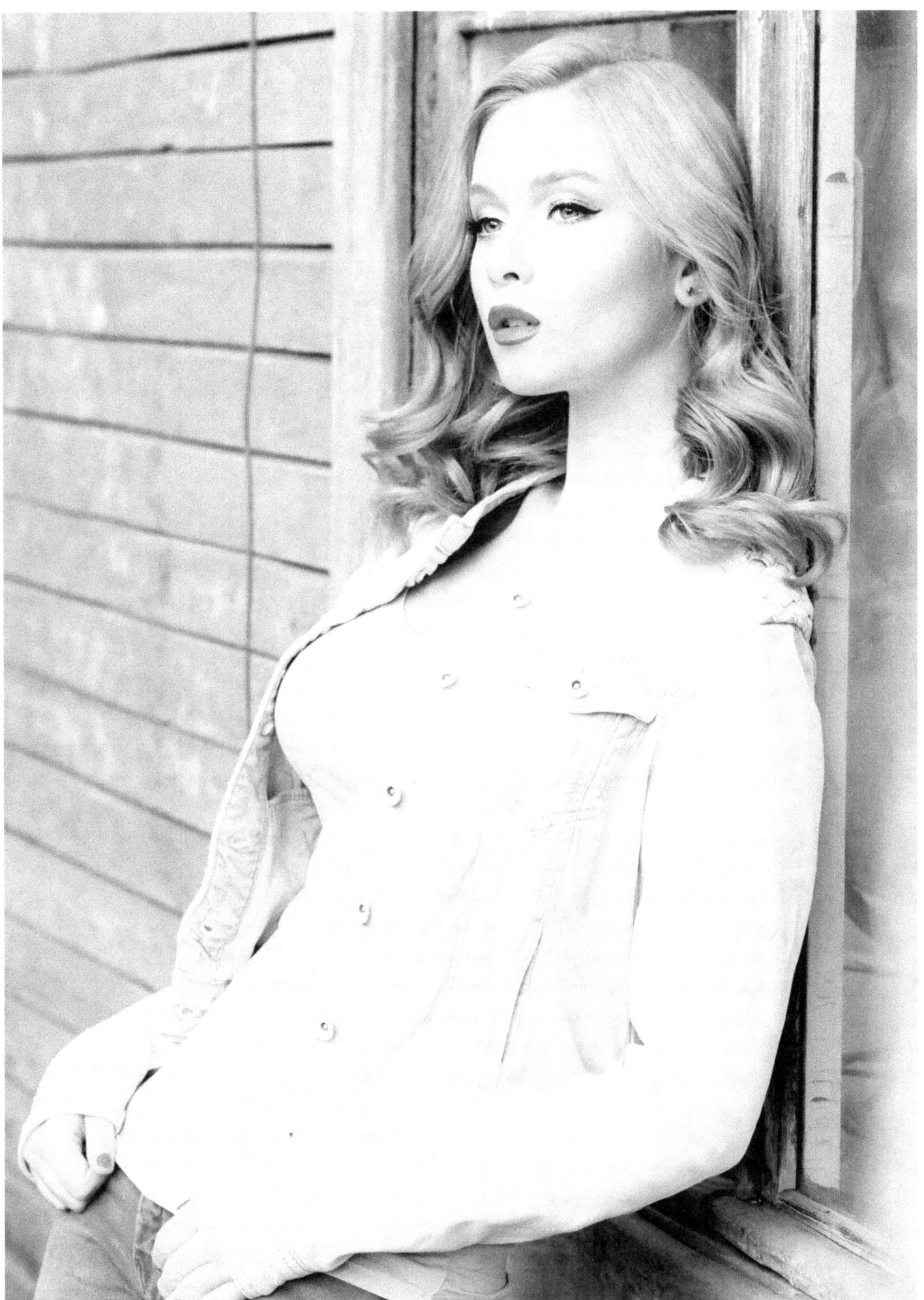

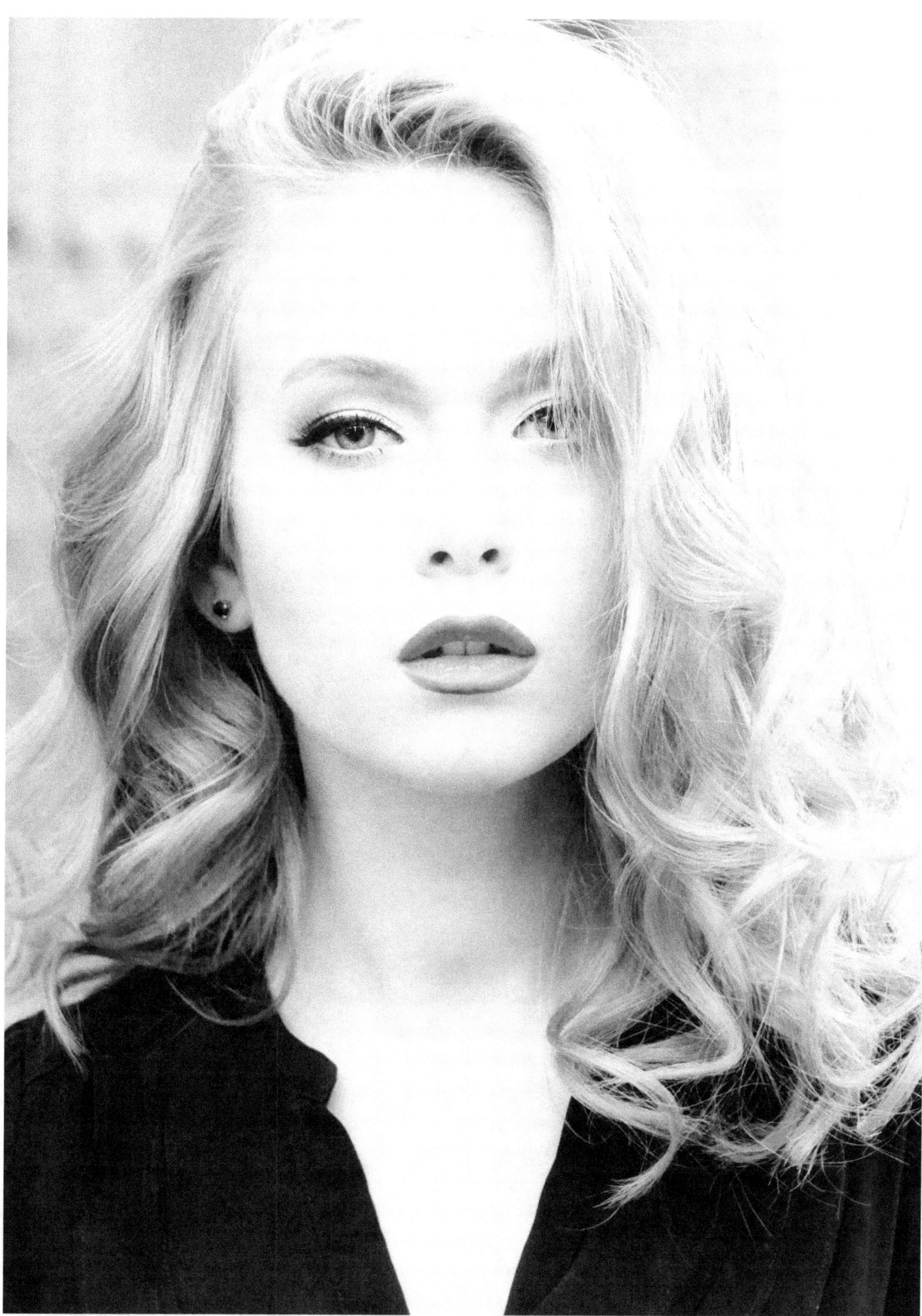

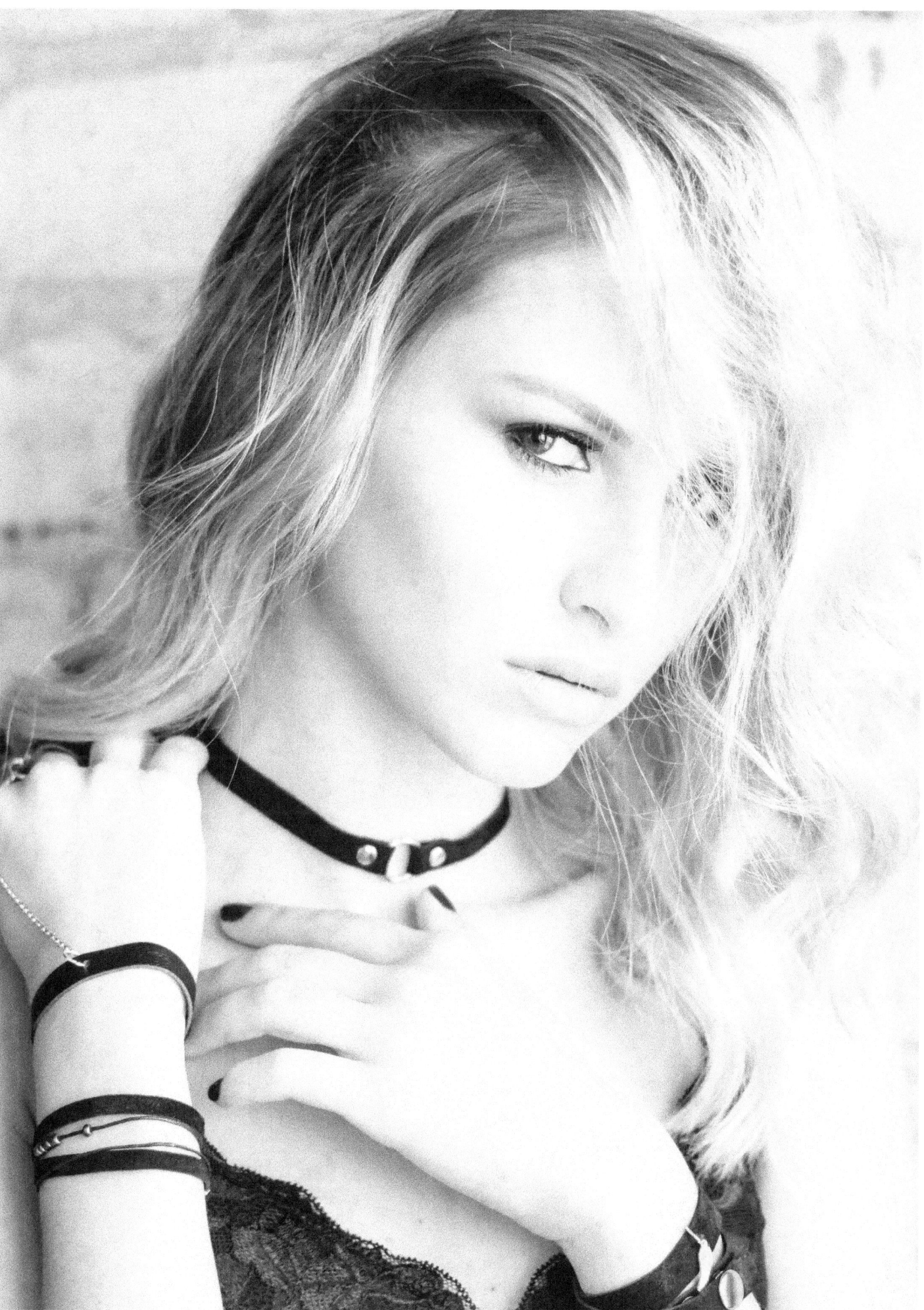

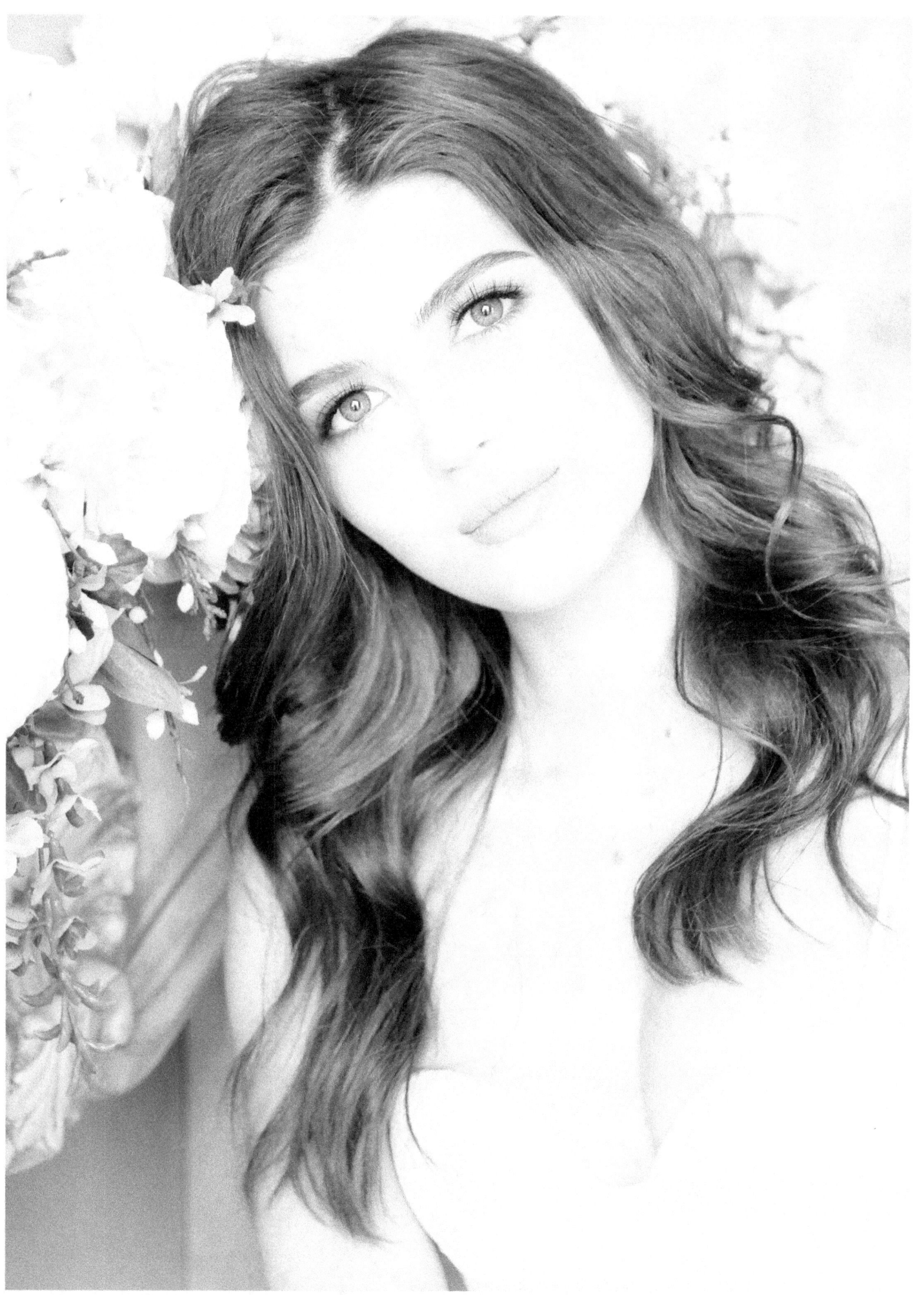

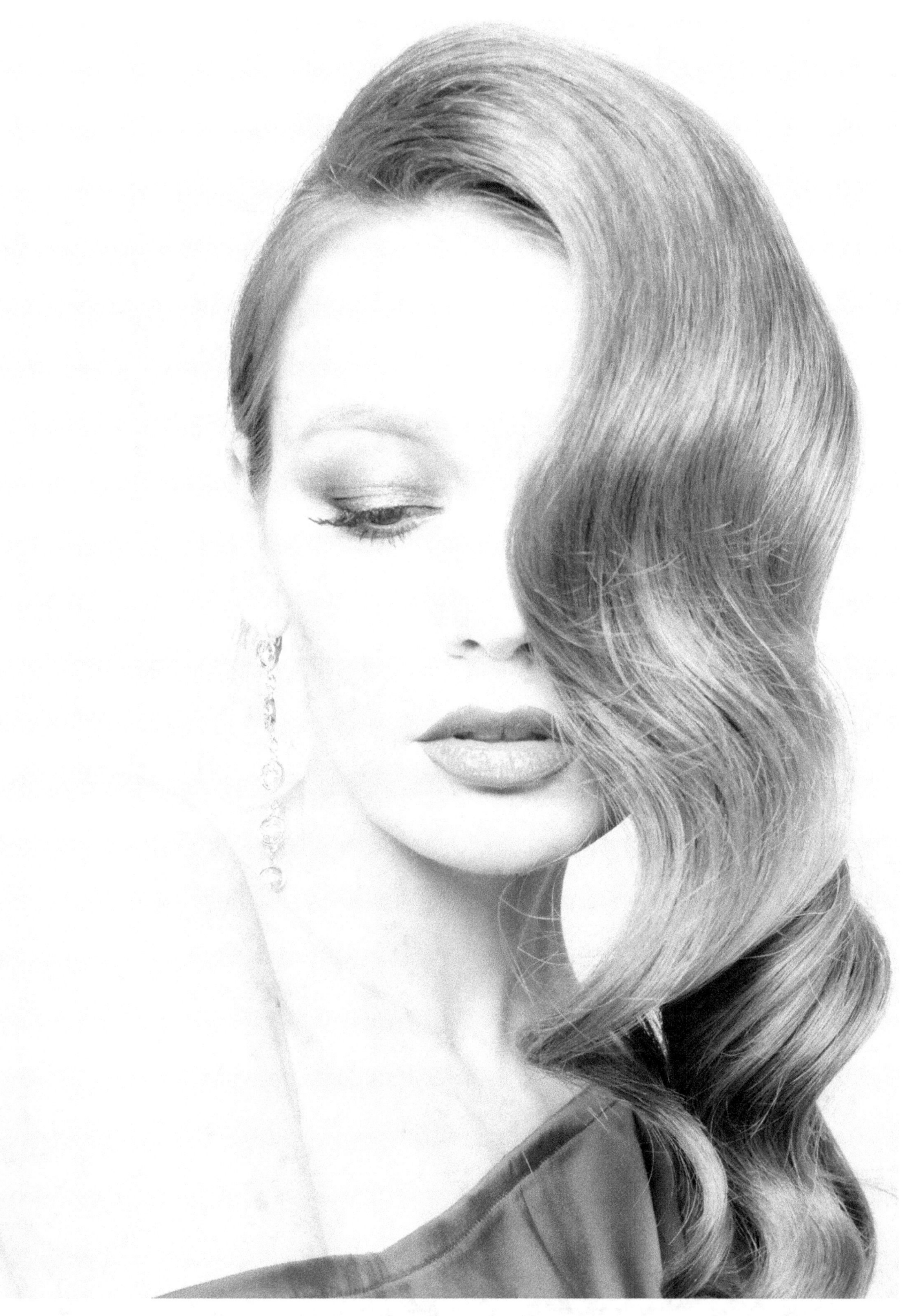

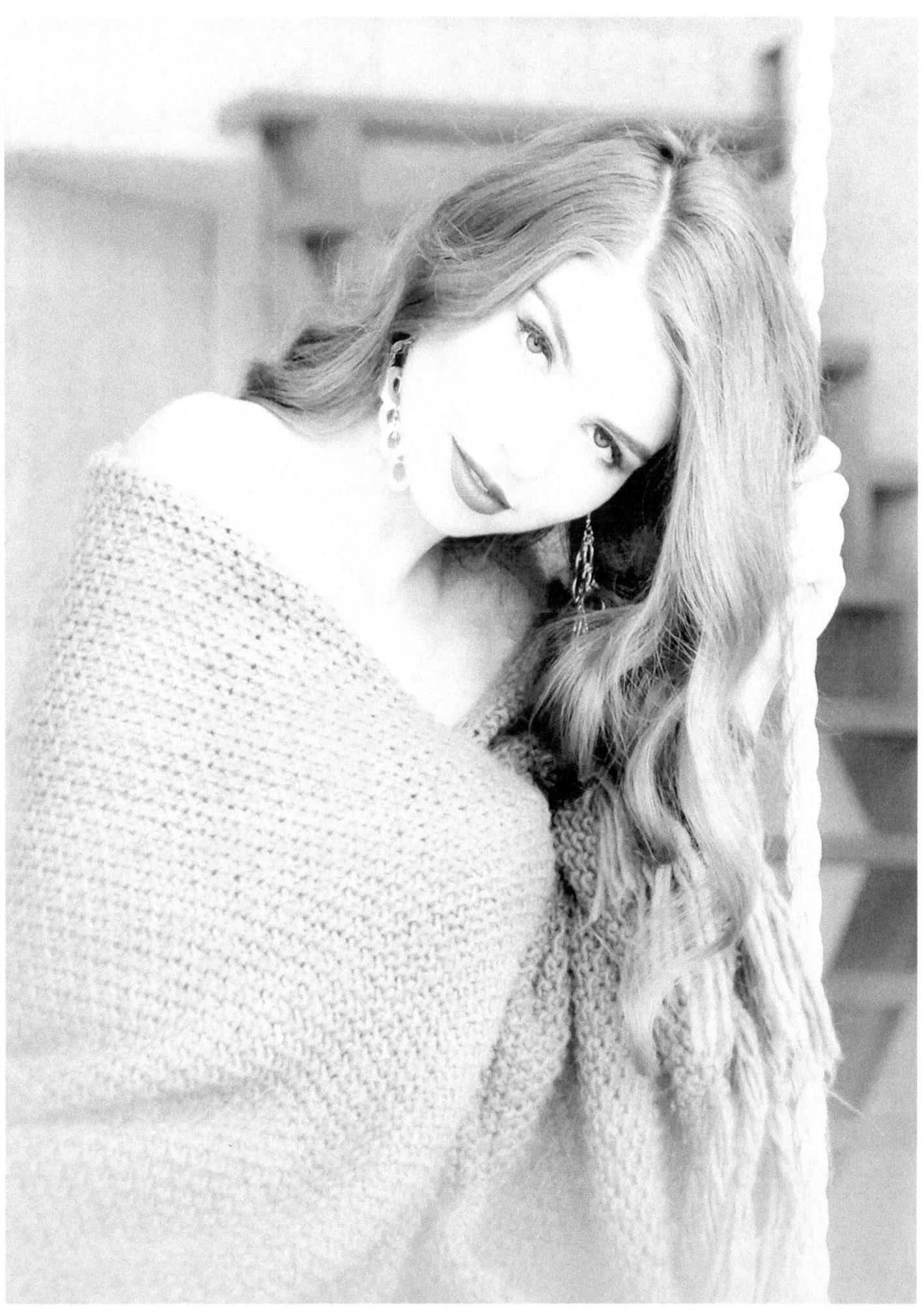

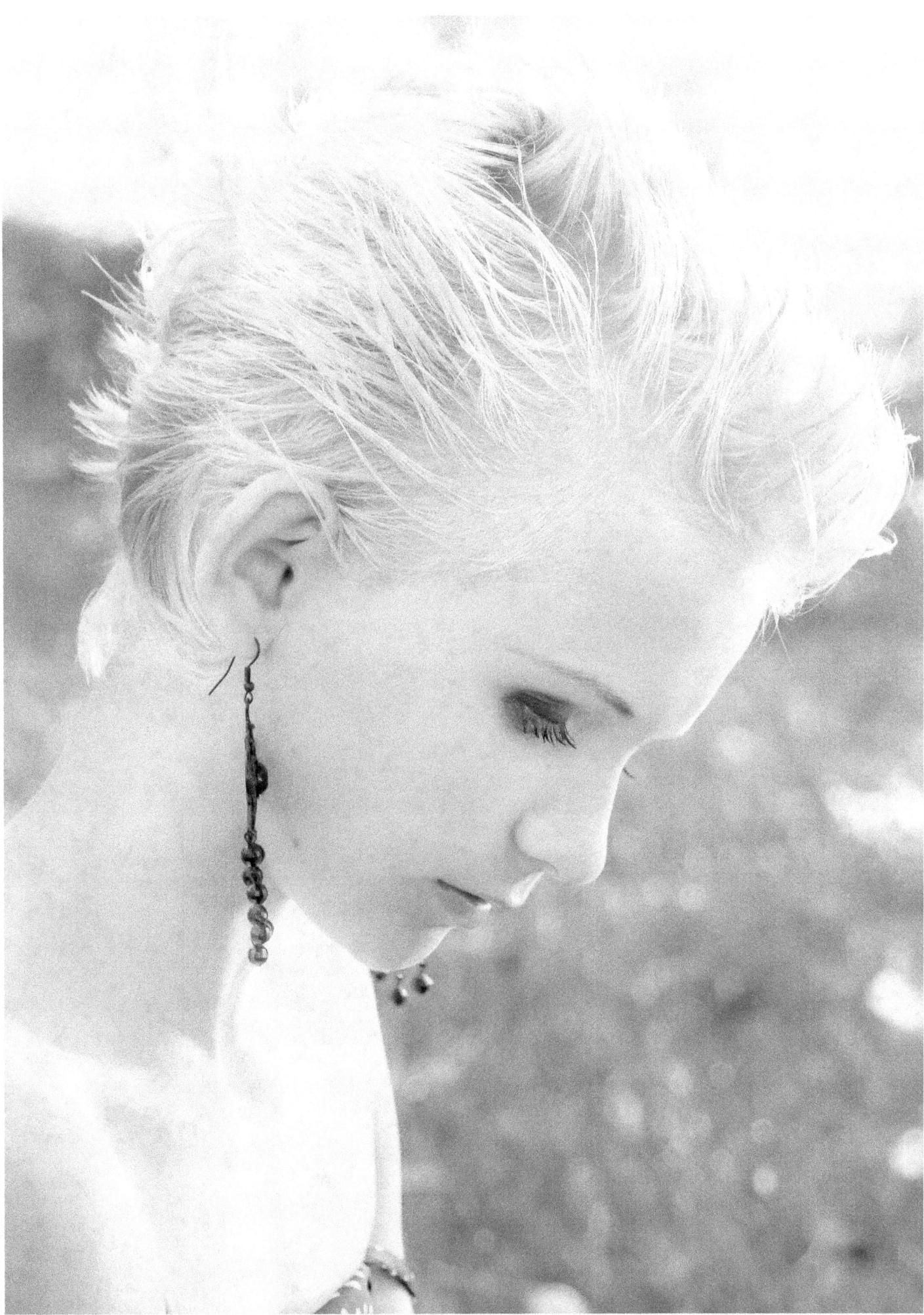

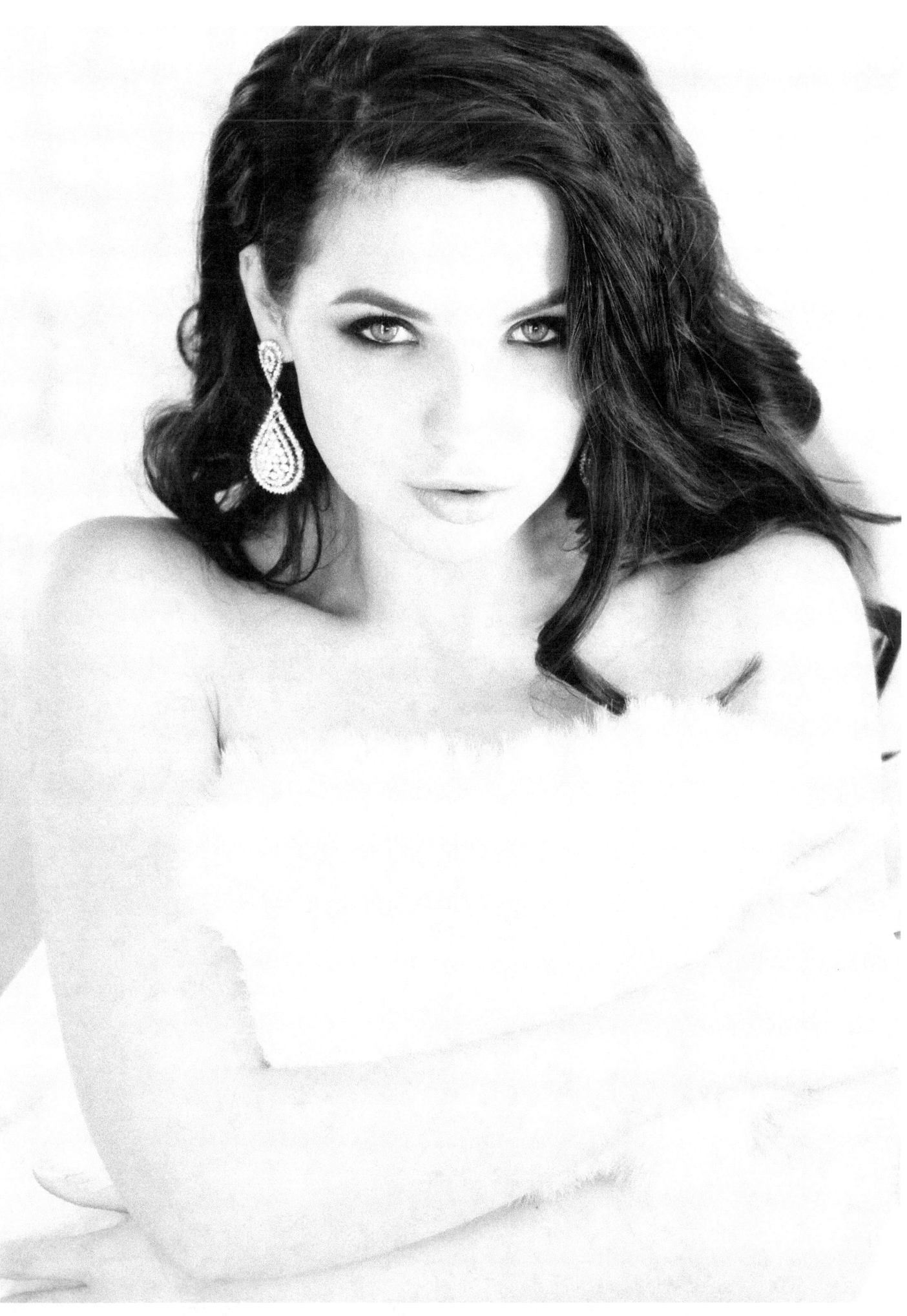

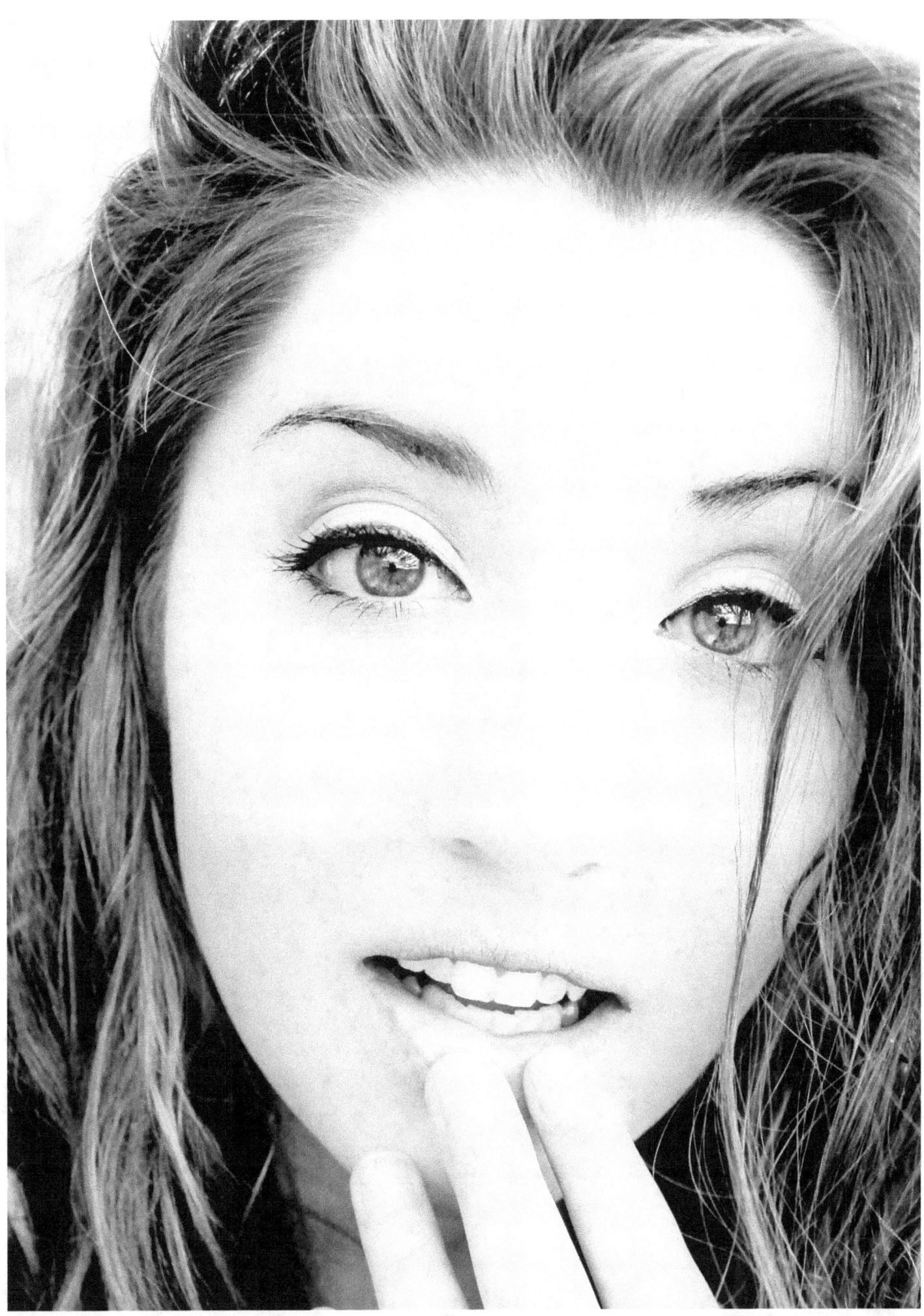

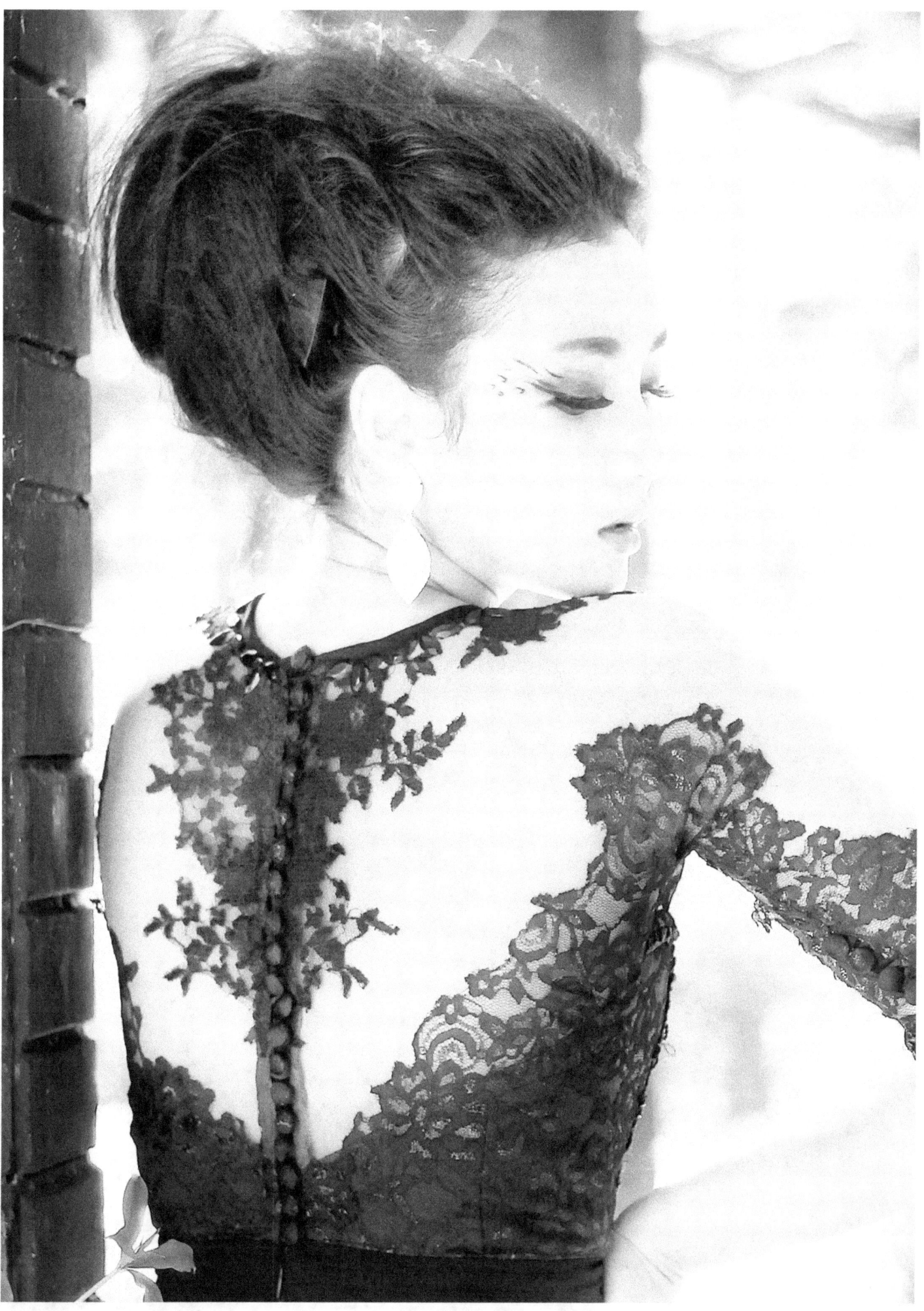

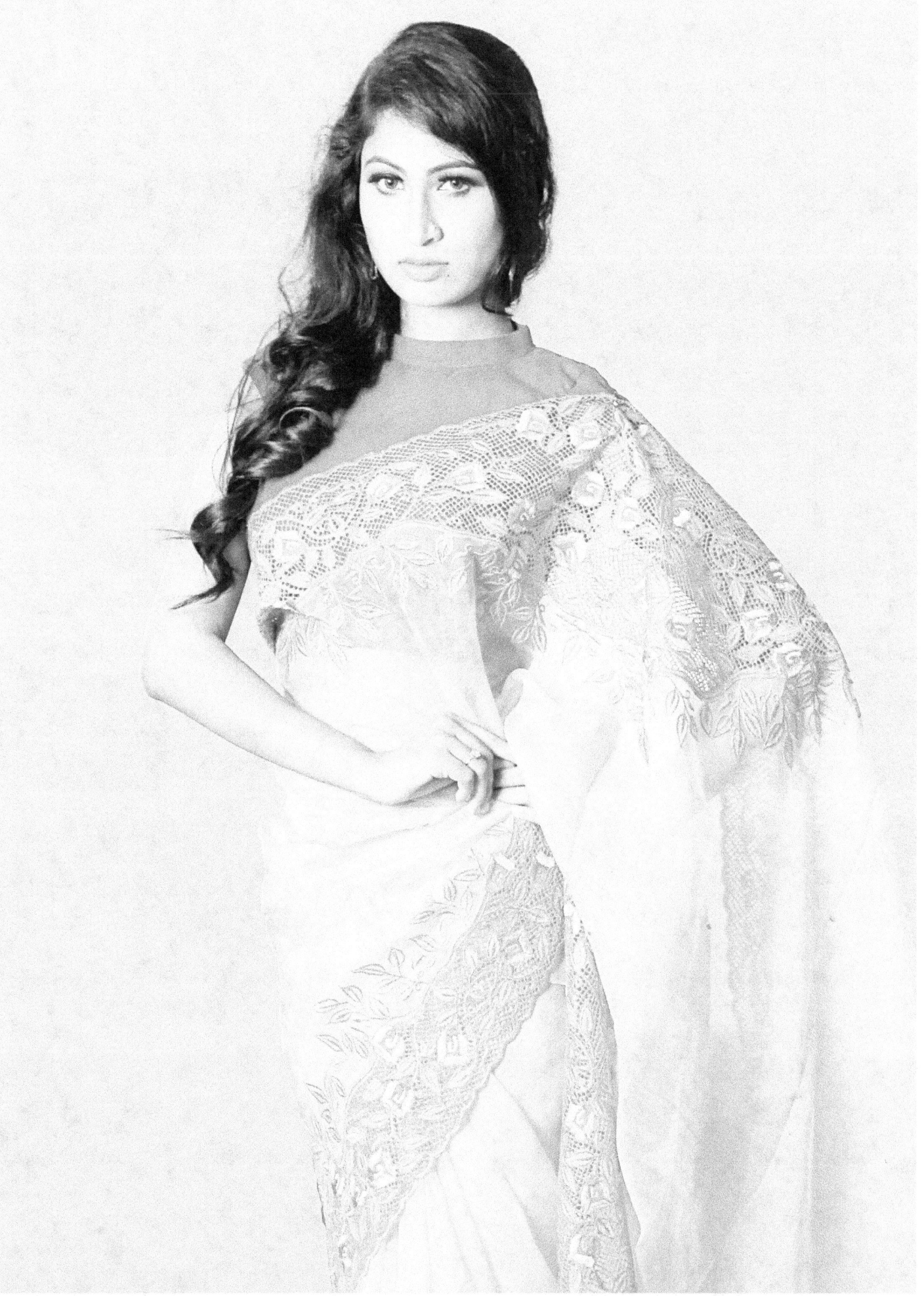

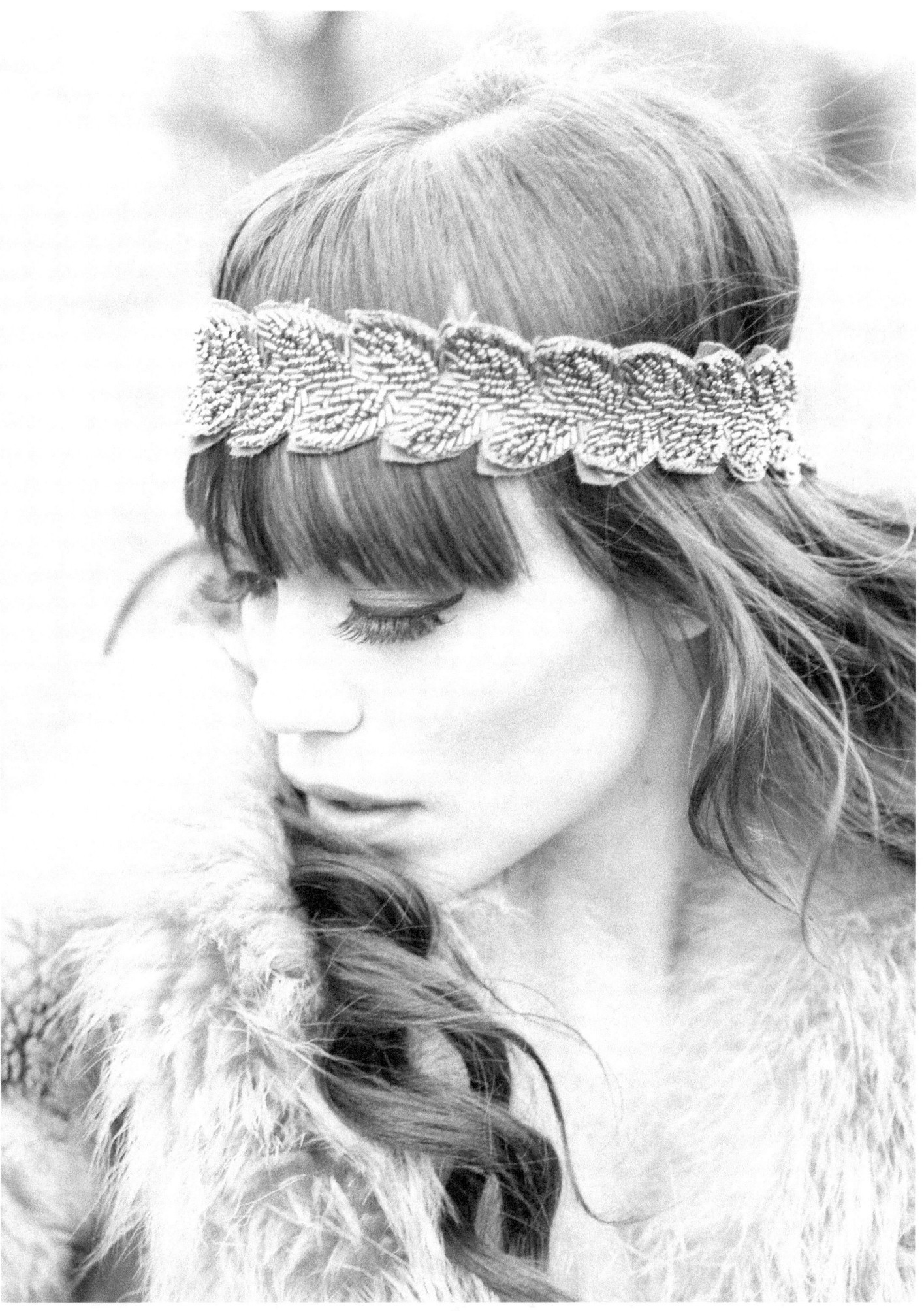

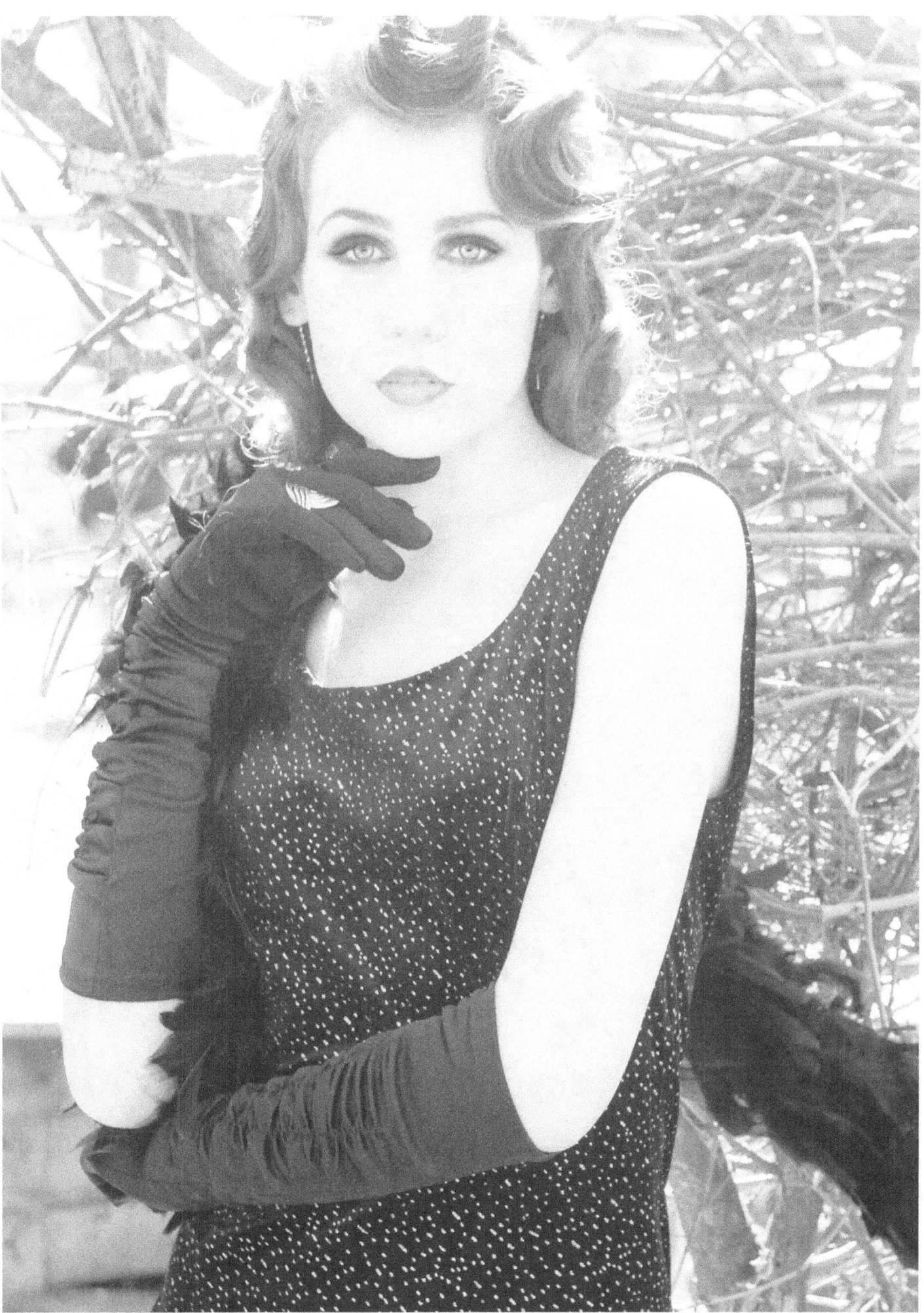

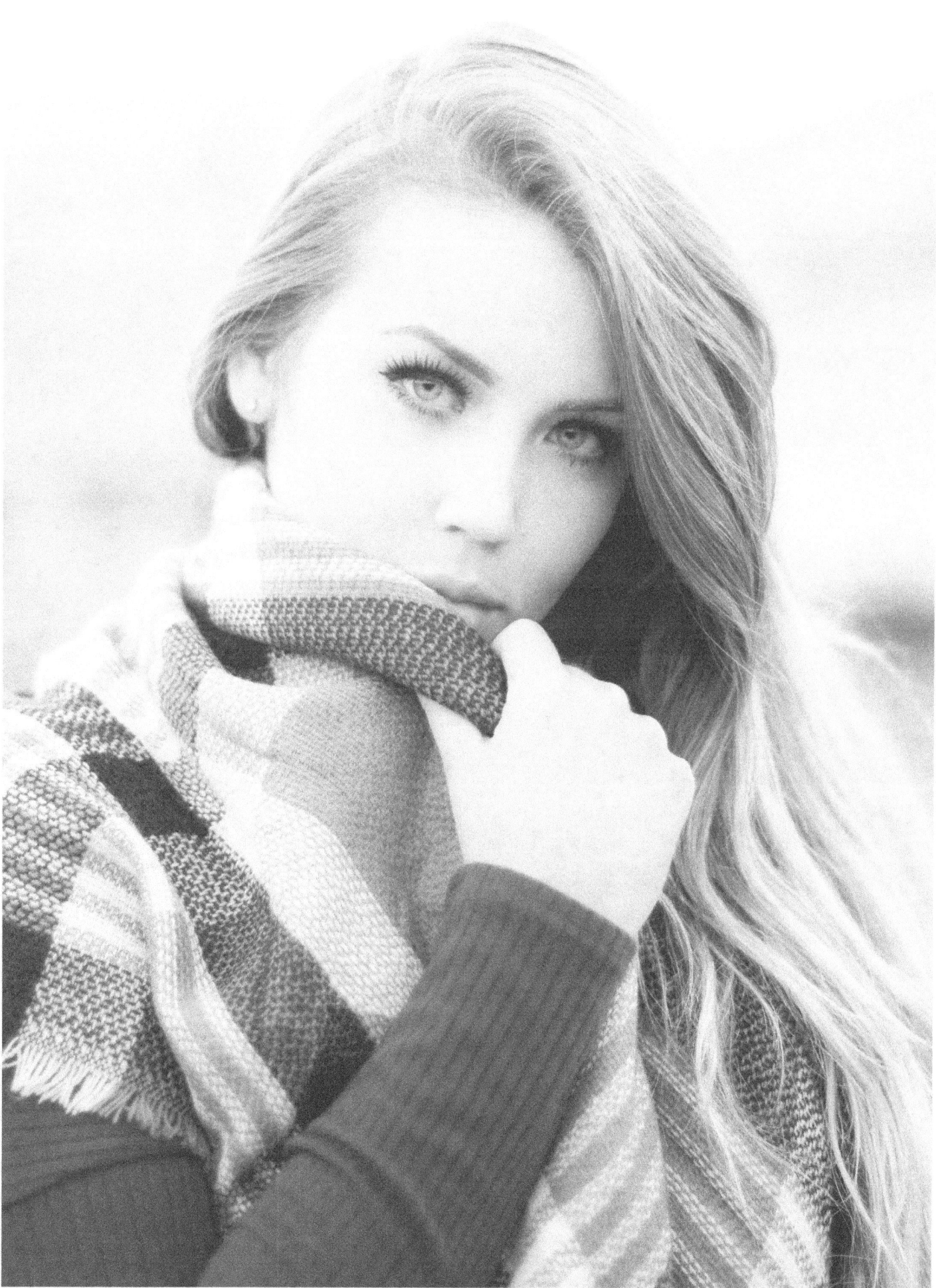

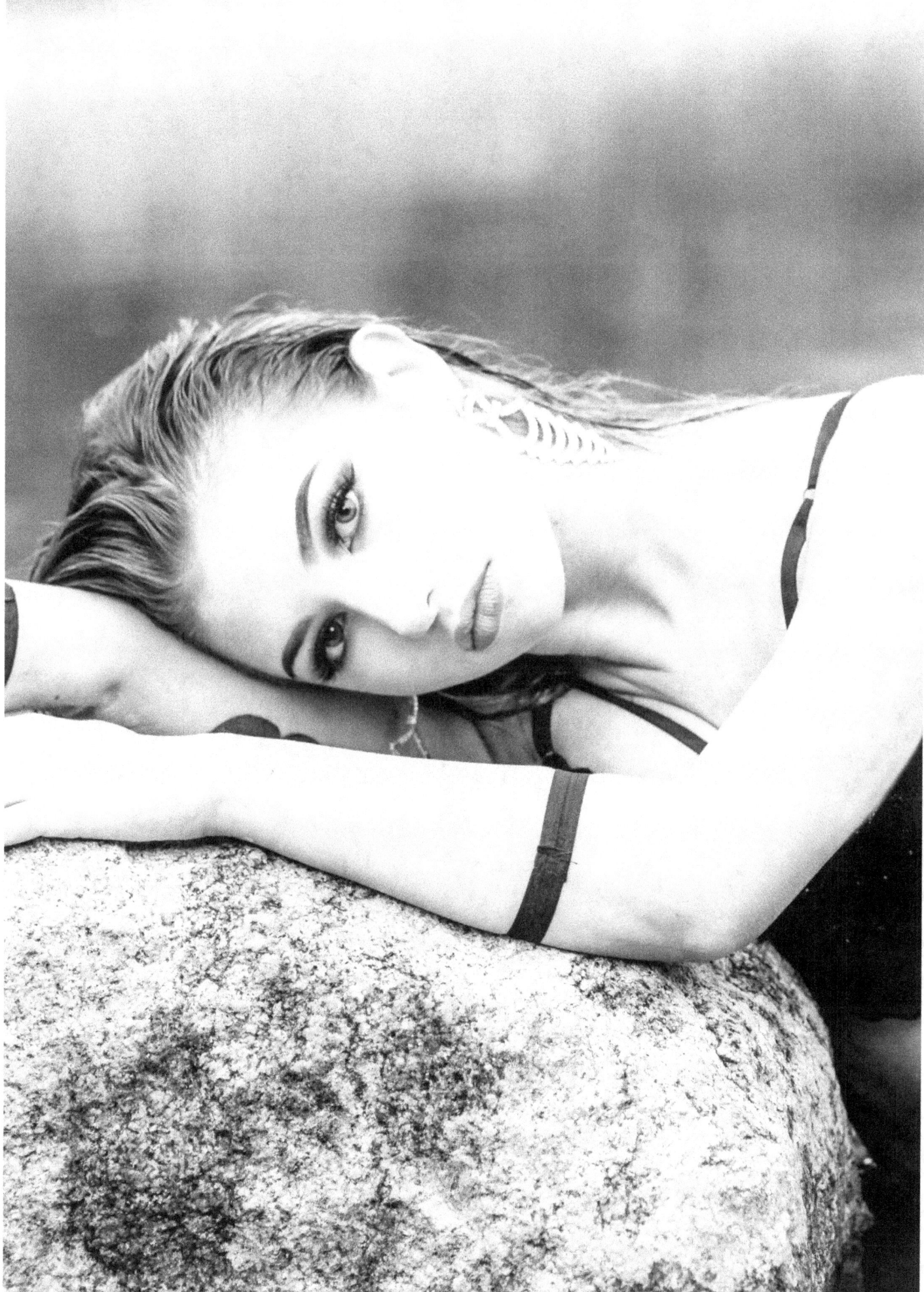

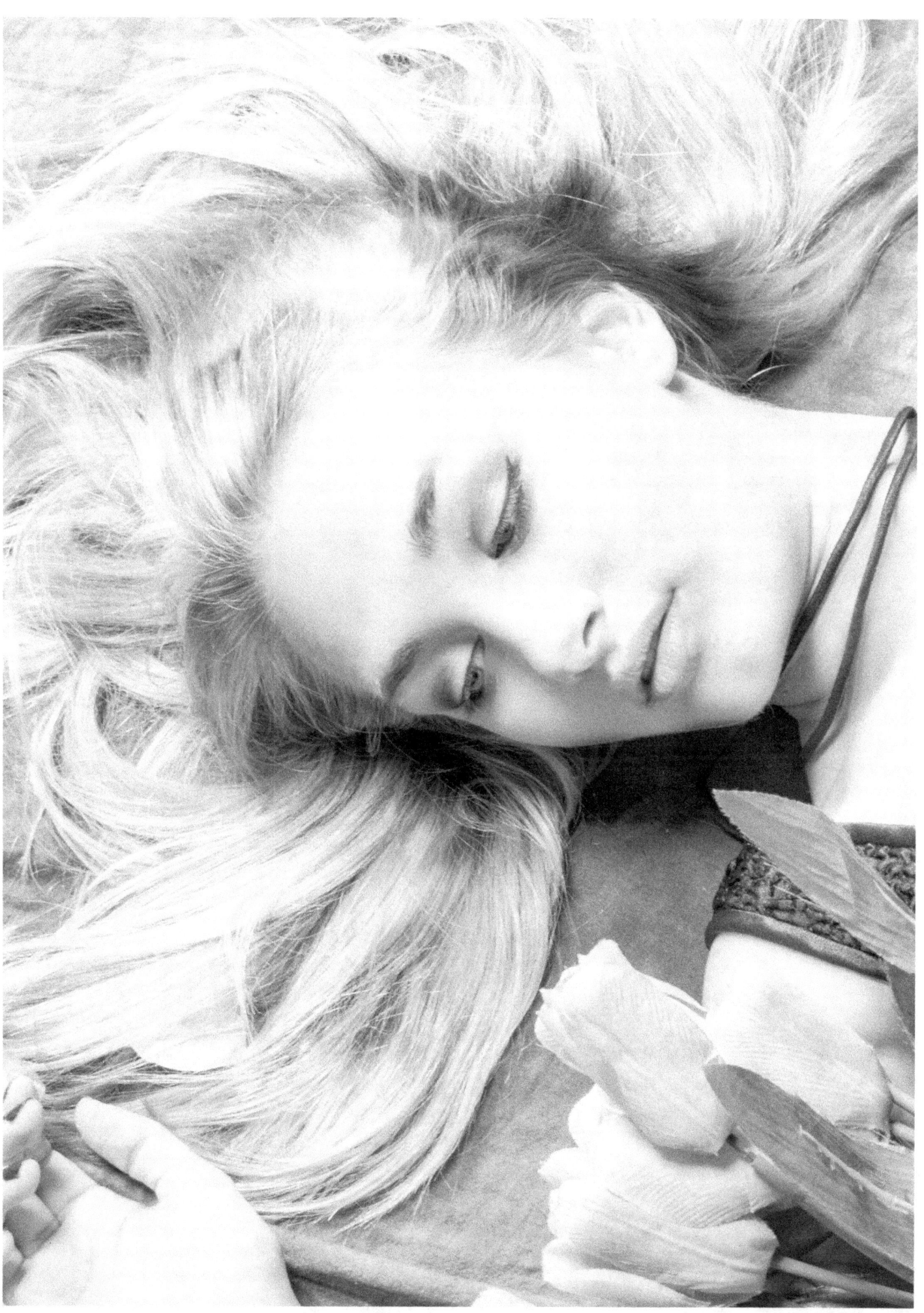

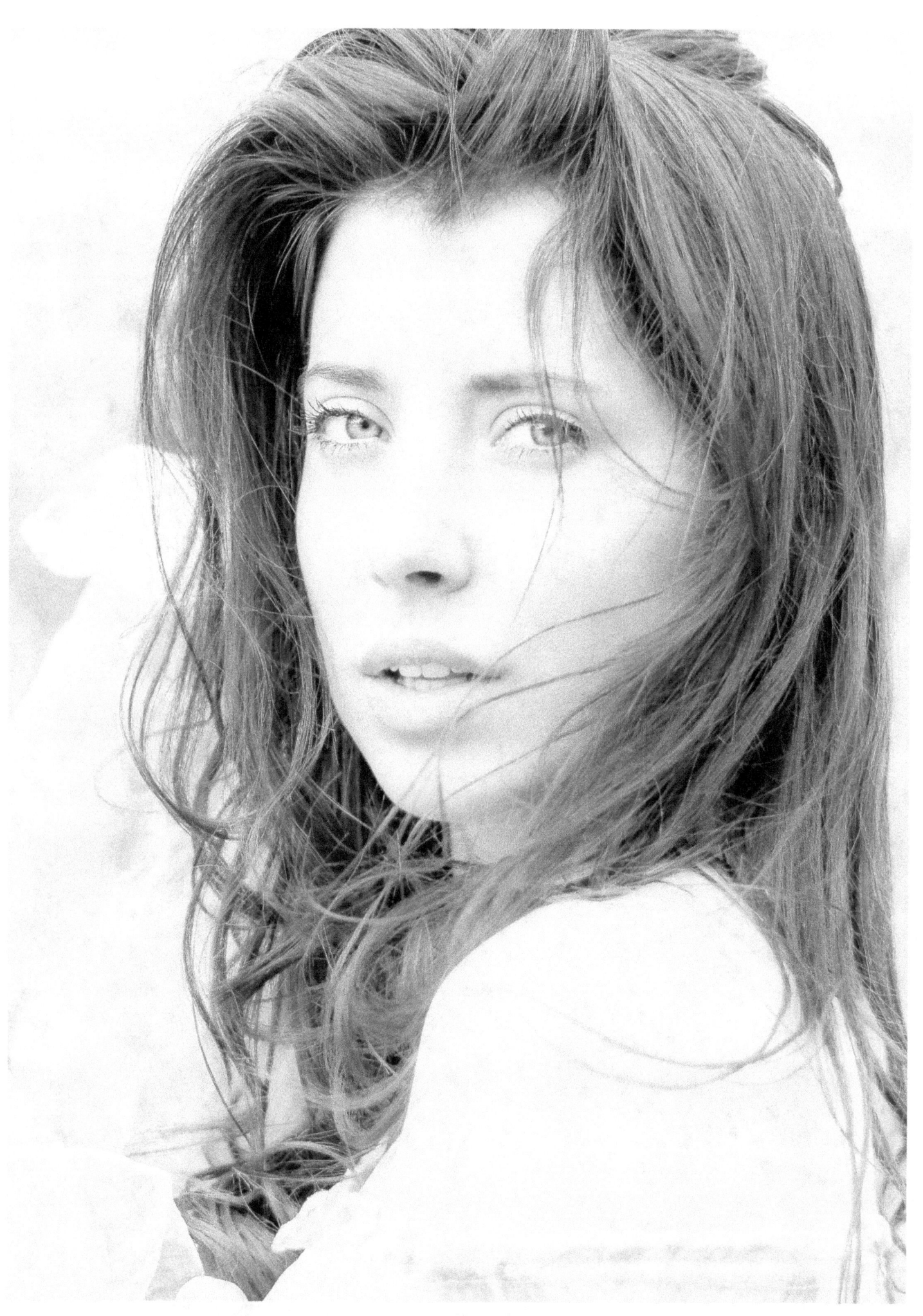

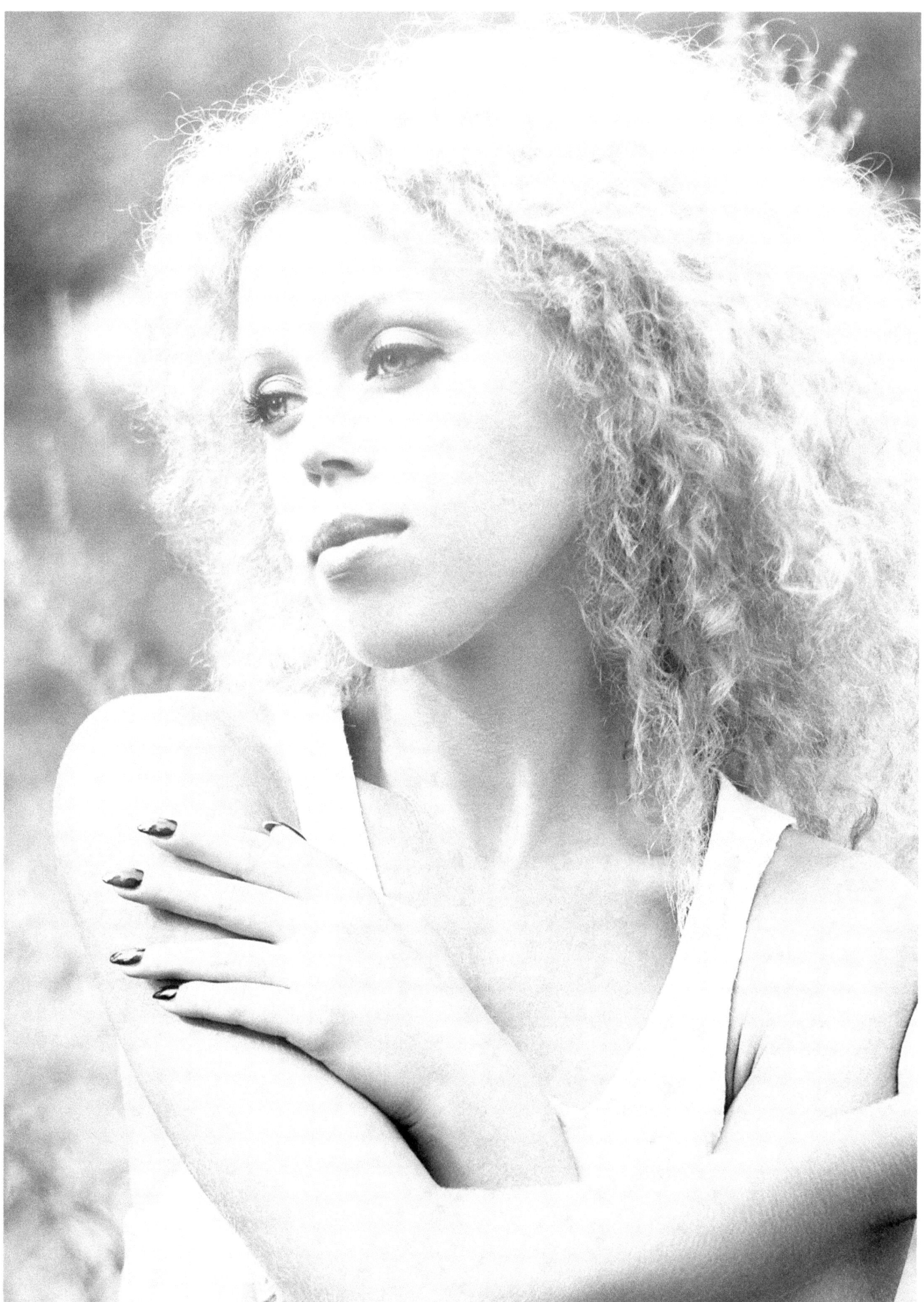

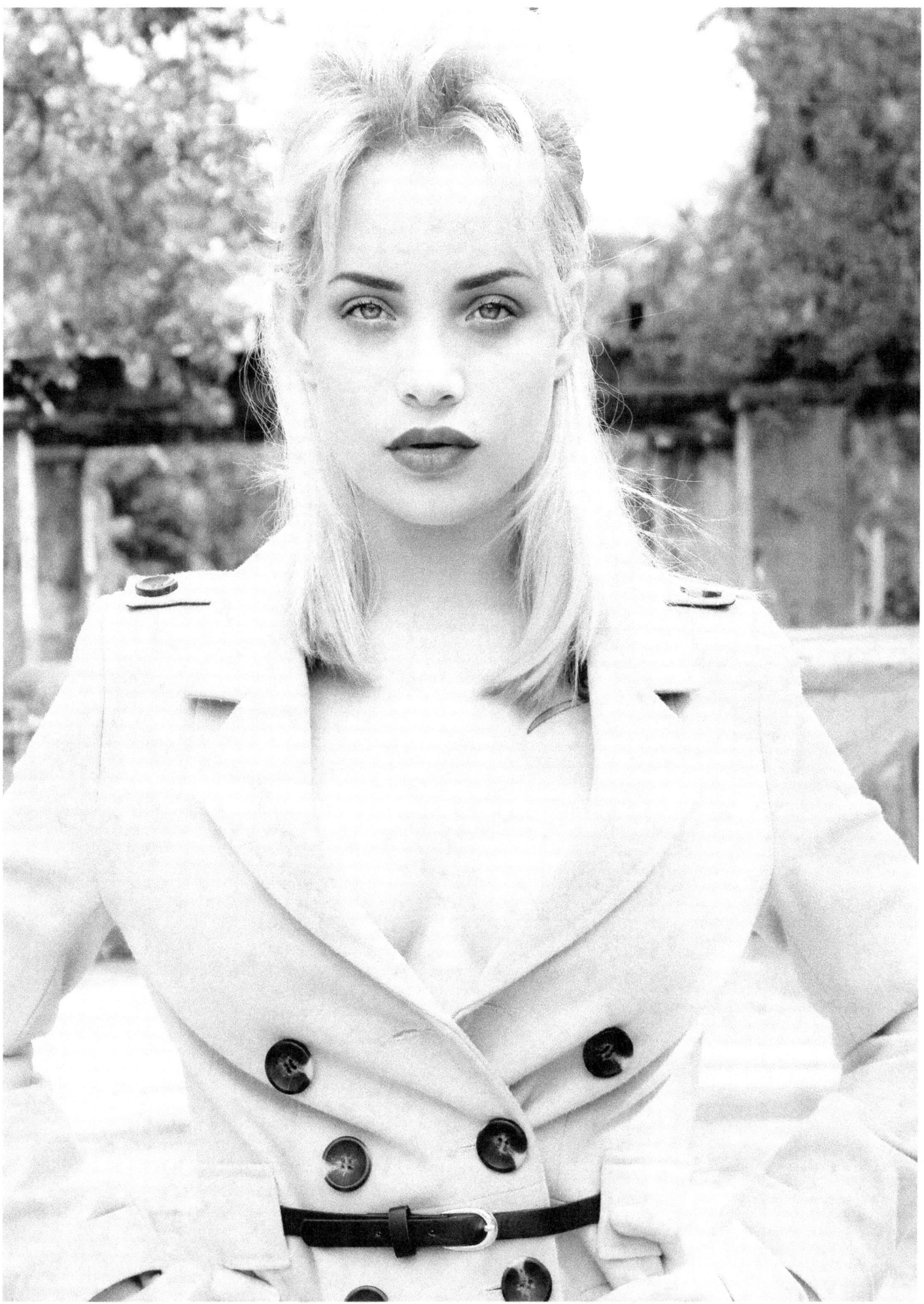

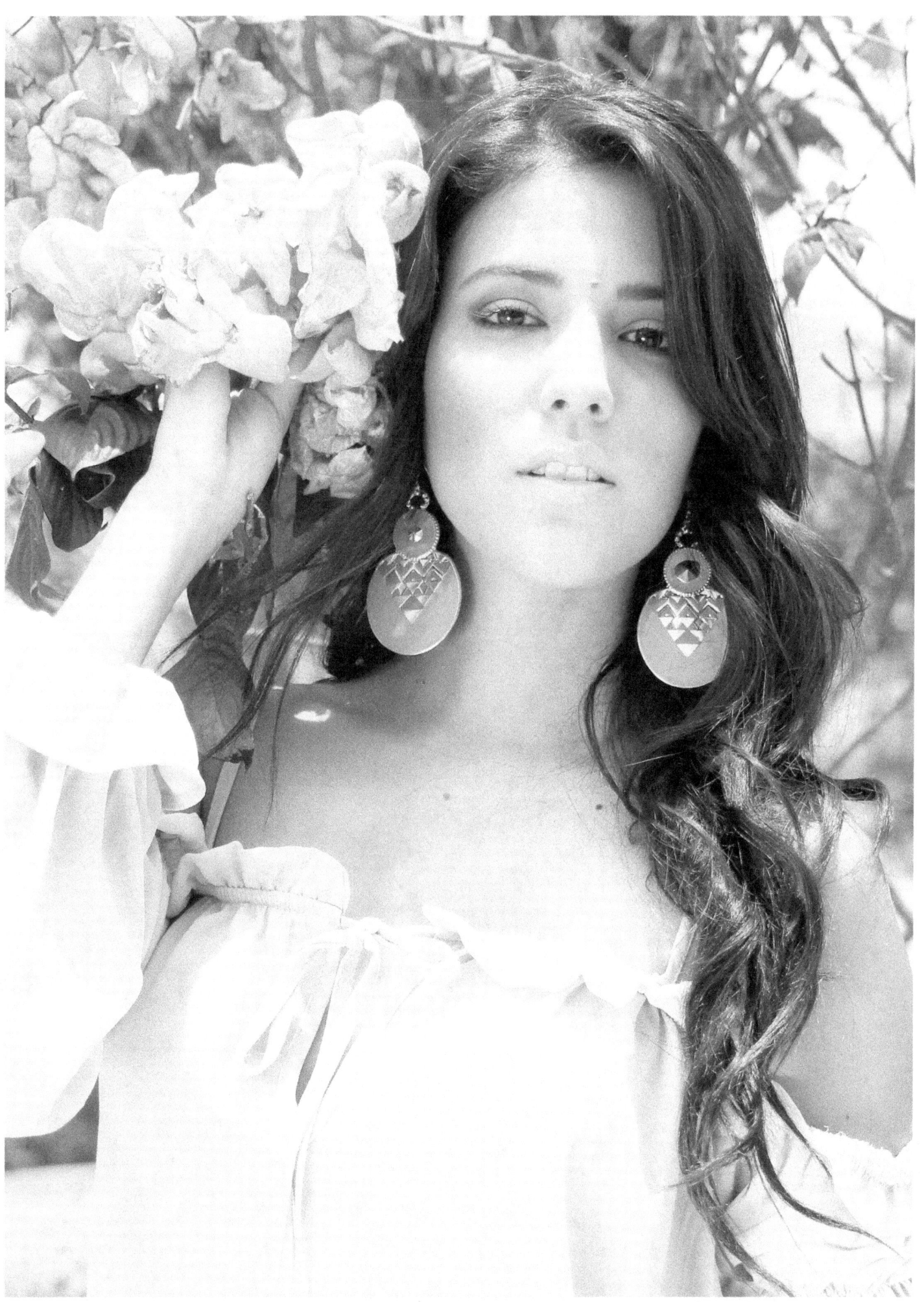

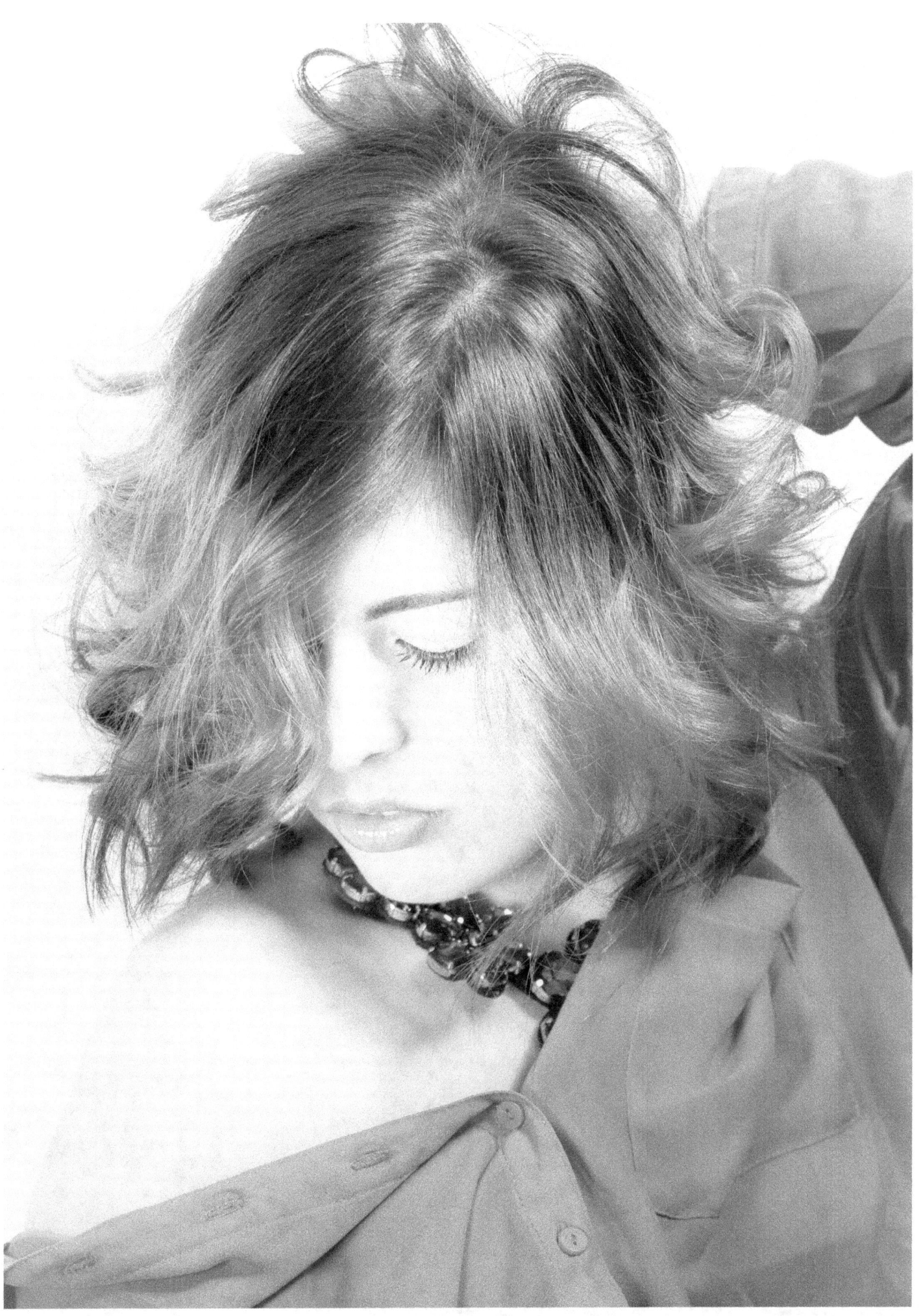

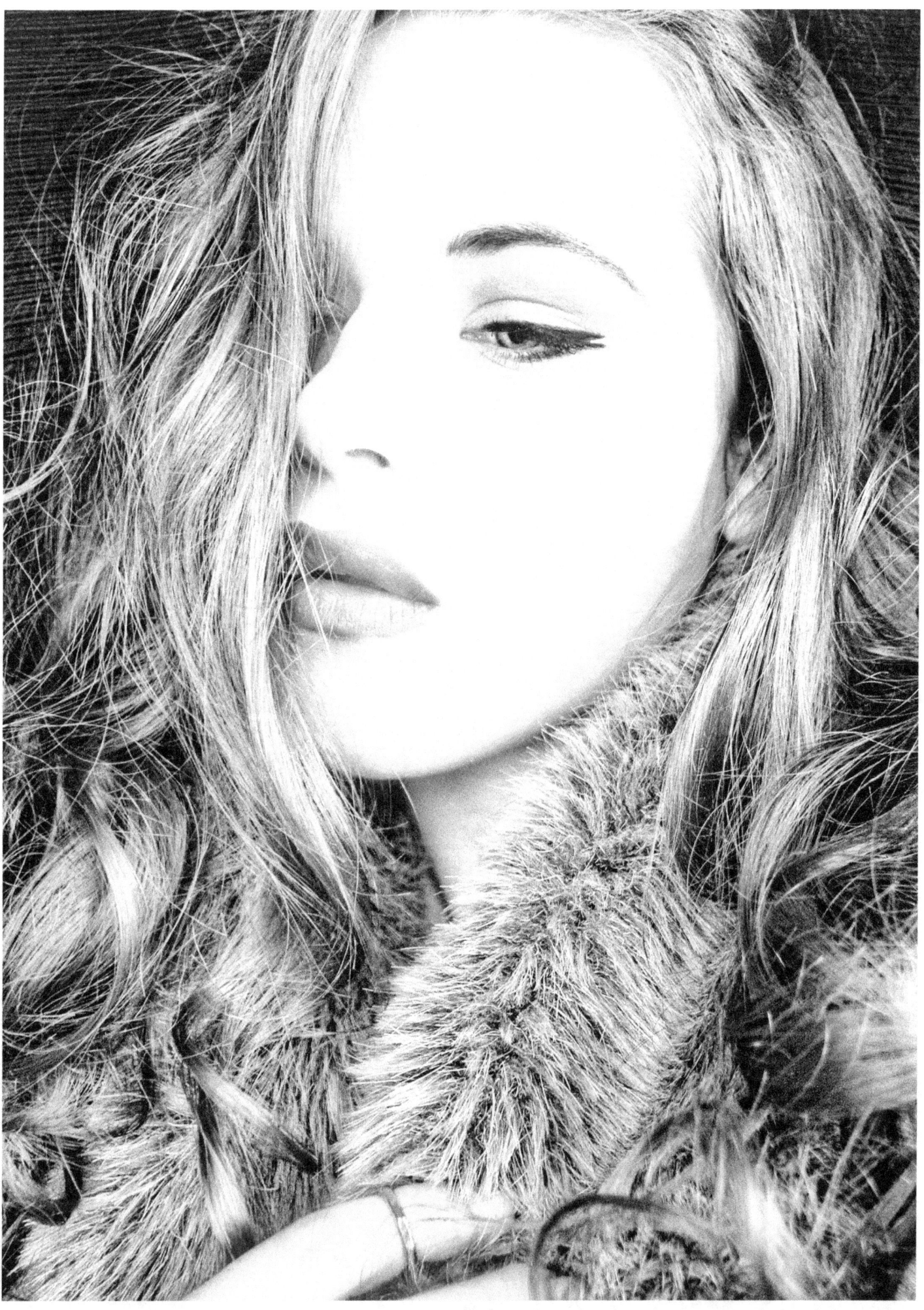

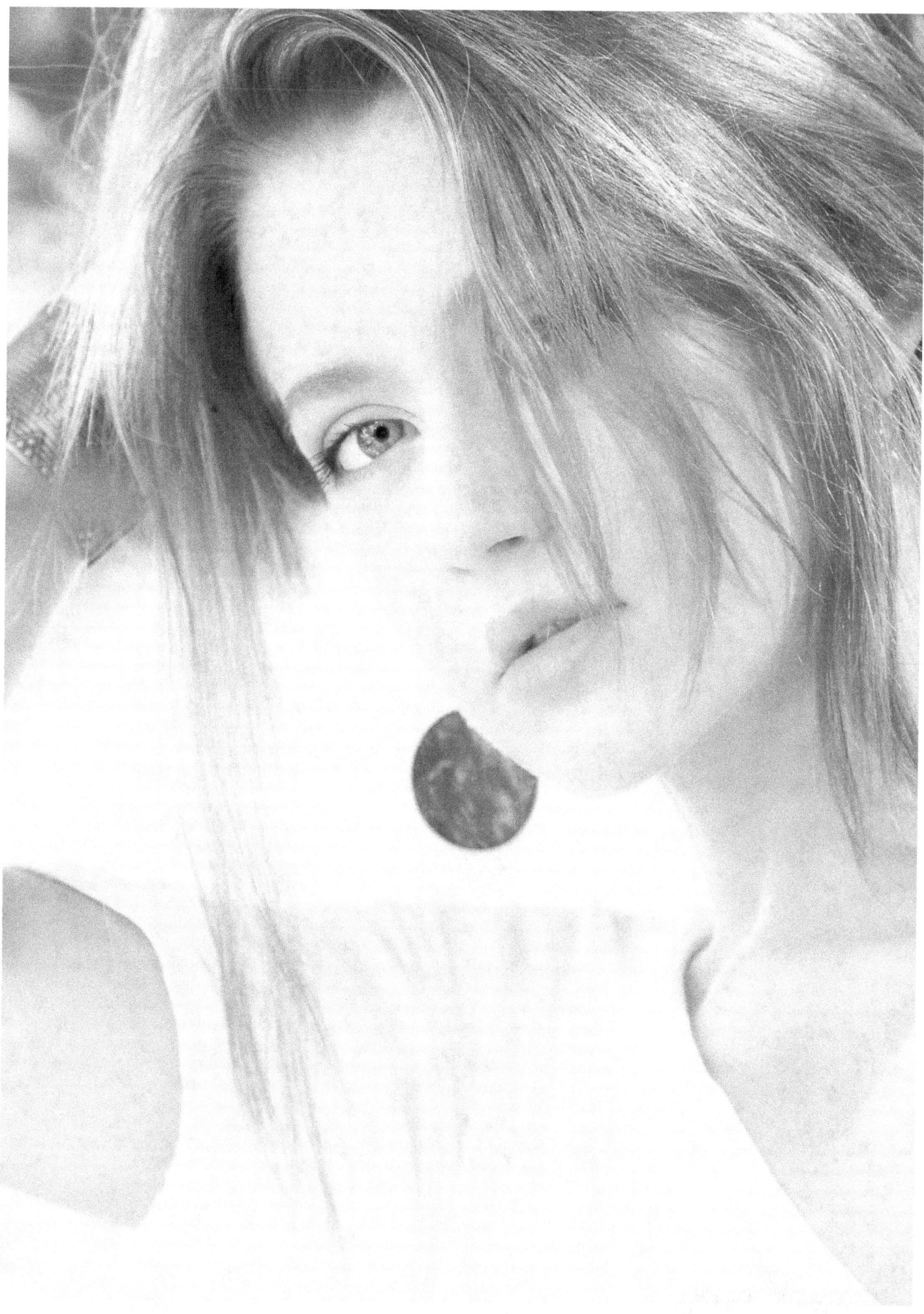

www.ingramcontent.com/pod-product-compliance
Lightning Source LLC
Chambersburg PA
CBHW081306180526
45170CB00007B/2585